Mel Bay's
Banjo G Tuning
Photo Chord Book

Online Video

Video
dv.melbay.com/20297
You Tube
www.melbay.com/20297V

3 4 5 6 7 8 9 0

Visit us on the Web at www.melbay.com — E-mail us at email@melbay.com

TUNING THE BANJO

G - BLUEGRASS

The 5 strings are tuned to a piano as shown.

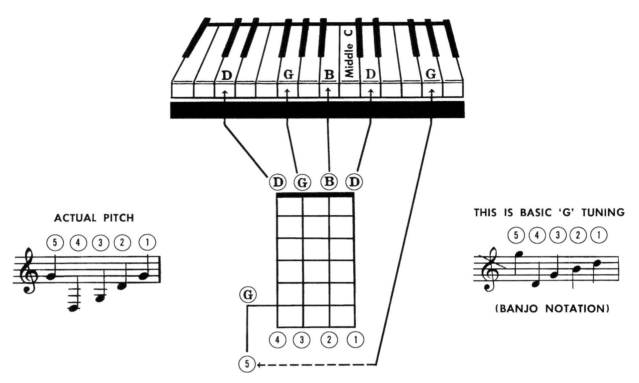

ACTUAL PITCH

THIS IS BASIC 'G' TUNING

(BANJO NOTATION)

Banjo music written an octave higher than the actual sound, will be indicated by

When the music is written exactly as heard, it will be indicated by

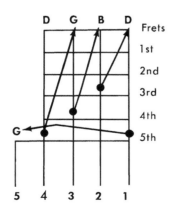

◄— ANOTHER WAY TO TUNE

Tune the first string to 'D' (Next above middle C)

Tune 2nd string, noted at 3rd fret, to same pitch as open first string.

Tune 3rd string, noted at 4th fret, to same pitch as open second string.

Tune the 5th string, to sound the same as the 1st string noted at the 5th fret.

Table of Contents

C Major*

Root - 3rd - 5th
C - E - G

C

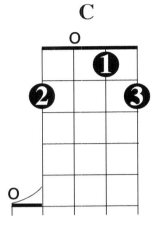

C Minor

Root - ♭3rd - 5th
C - E♭ - G

Cm

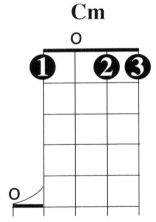

C Seventh

Root - 3rd - 5th - ♭7th
C - E - G - B♭

C7

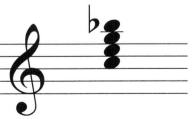

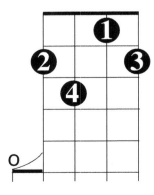

*notational spelling
not necessarily the
same as voicing of
pictured chord inversion.

C Chords

C Diminished

Root - ♭3rd - ♭5th - ♭♭7th
C - E♭ - G♭ - B♭♭

C° or Cdim

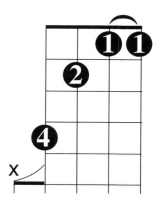

C Augmented

Root - 3rd - ♯5th
C - E - G♯

C+ or Caug

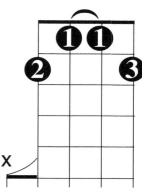

C Sixth

Root - 3rd - 5th - 6th
C - E - G - A

C6

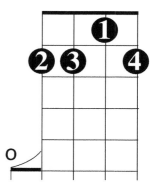

C Chords

C Minor Sixth

Root - ♭3rd - 5th - 6th
C - E♭ - G - A

Cm6

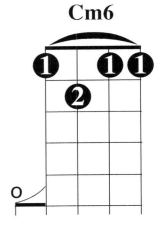

C Seven Flat Five

Root - 3rd - ♭5th - ♭7th
C - E - G♭ - B♭

C7♭5

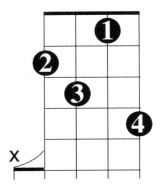

C Major Seventh

Root - 3rd - 5th - 7th
C - E - G - B

CMaj7

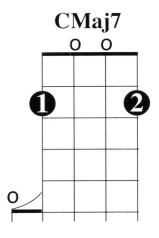

C Chords

C Major Seventh Flat Third

Root - ♭3rd - 5th - 7th
C - E♭ - G - B

CMaj7♭3

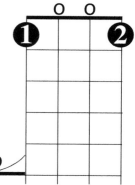

C Minor Seventh

Root - ♭3rd - 5th - ♭7th
C - E♭ - G - B♭

Cm7

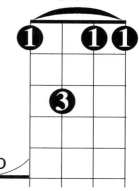

C Minor Seventh Flat Five*

Root - ♭3rd - ♭5th - ♭7th
C - E♭ - G♭ - B♭

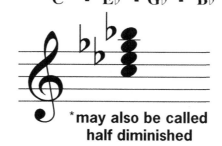

*may also be called
half diminished

Cm7♭5

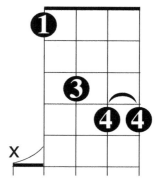

C Seventh Suspended Fourth

Root - 4th - 5th - ♭7th
C - F - G - B♭

C7sus

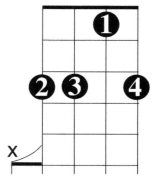

7

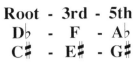

D♭ Major

Root - 3rd - 5th
D♭ - F - A♭
C♯ - E♯ - G♯

D♭

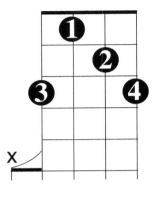

D♭ Minor

Root - ♭3rd - 5th
D♭ - F♭ - A♭
C♯ - E♮ - G♯

D♭m

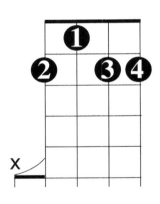

D♭ Seventh

Root - 3rd - 5th - ♭7th
D♭ - F - A♭ - C♭
C♯ - E♯ - G♯ - B

D♭7

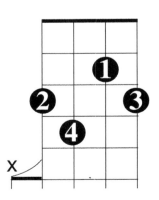

D♭ Diminished

Root - ♭3rd - ♭5th - ♭♭7th
D♭ - F♭ - A♭♭ - C♭♭
C♯ - E - G - B♭

D♭o

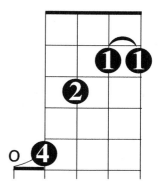

D♭ Augmented

Root - 3rd - ♯5th
D♭ - F - A♮
C♯ - E♯ - G𝄪

D♭+

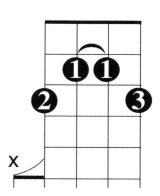

D♭ Sixth

Root - 3rd - 5th - 6th
D♭ - F - A♭ - B♭
C♯ - E♯ - G♯ - A♯

D♭6

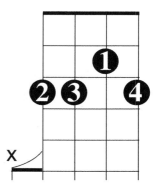

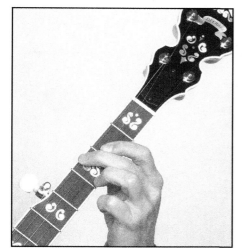

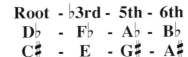

D♭ Minor Sixth

Root - ♭3rd - 5th - 6th
D♭ - F♭ - A♭ - B♭
C♯ - E - G♯ - A♯

D♭m6

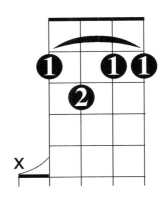

D♭ Seven Flat Five

Root - 3rd - ♭5th - ♭7th
D♭ - F - A♭♭ - C♭
C♯ - E♯ - G♮ - B

D♭7♭5

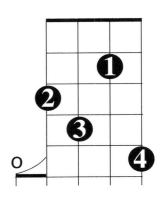

D♭ Major Seventh

Root - 3rd - 5th - 7th
D♭ - F - A♭ - C
C♯ - E♯ - G♯ - B♯

D♭Maj7

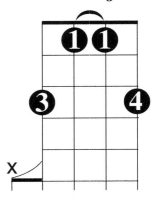

Db Major Seventh Flat Third

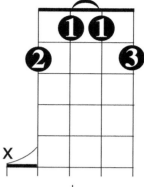

DbMaj7b3

Root - b3rd - 5th - 7th
Db - Fb - Ab - C
C# - E - G# - B#

Db Minor Seventh

Dbm7

Root - b3rd - 5th - b7th
Db - Fb - Ab - Cb
C# - E - G# - B♮

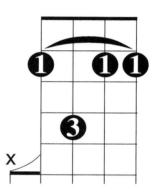

Db Minor Seventh Flat Five

Dbm7b5

Root - b3rd - b5th - b7th
Db - Fb - Abb - Cb
C# - E - G - B

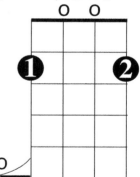

Db Seventh Suspended Fourth

Db7sus

Root - 4th - 5th - b7th
Db - Gb - Ab - Cb
C# - F# - G# - B

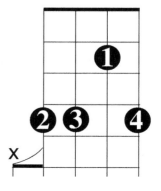

D Major

Root - 3rd - 5th
D - F# - A

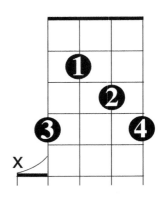

D

D Minor

Root - b3rd - 5th
D - F♮ - A

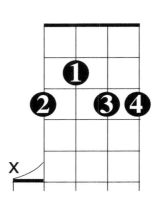

Dm

D Seventh

Root - 3rd - 5th - b7th
D - F# - A - C♮

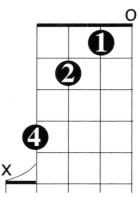

D7

D Chords

D Diminished

Root - ♭3rd - ♭5th - ♭♭7th
D - F♯ - A♭ - C♭

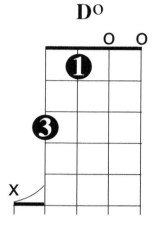

D°

D Augmented

Root - 3rd - ♯5th
D - F♯ - A♯

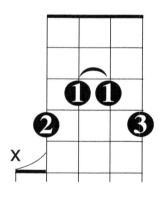

D+

D Sixth

Root - 3rd - 5th - 6th
D - F♯ - A - B

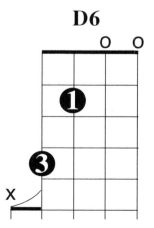

D6

D Minor Sixth

Root - ♭3rd - 5th - 6th
D - F♮ - A - B

Dm6

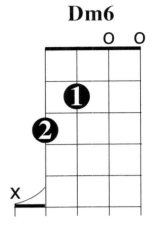

D Seven Flat Five

Root - 3rd - ♭5th - ♭7th
D - F♯ - A♭ - C♮

D7♭5

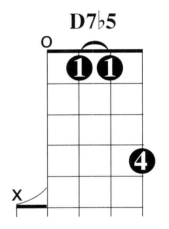

D Major Seventh

Root - 3rd - 5th - 7th
D - F♯ - A - C♯

DMaj7

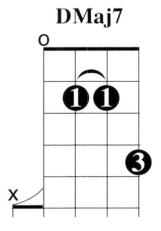

D Major Seventh Flat Third

DMaj7♭3

Root - ♭3rd - 5th - 7th
D - F♮ - A - C♯

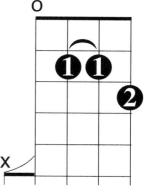

D Minor Seventh

Dm7

Root - ♭3rd - 5th - ♭7th
D - F♮ - A - C♮

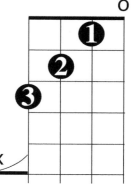

D Minor Seventh Flat Five

Dm7♭5

Root - ♭3rd - ♭5th - ♭7th
D - F♮ - A♭ - C♮

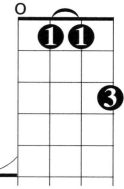

D Seventh Suspended Fourth

D7sus

Root - 4th - 5th - ♭7th
D - G - A - C♮

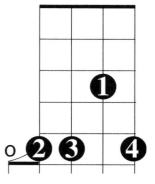

E♭ Major

Root - 3rd - 5th
E♭ - G - B♭

E♭

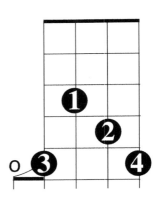

E♭ Minor

Root - ♭3rd - 5th
E♭ - G♭ - B♭

E♭m

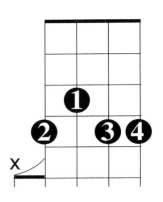

E♭ Seventh

Root - 3rd - 5th - ♭7th
E♭ - G - B♭ - D♭

E♭7

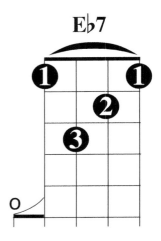

E♭ Diminished

Root - ♭3rd - ♭5th - ♭♭7th
E♭ - G♭ - B♭♭ - D♭♭

E♭°

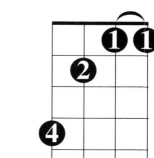

E♭ Augmented

Root - 3rd - ♯5th
E♭ - G - B♮

E♭+

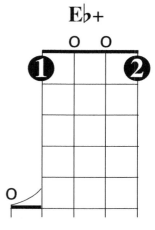

E♭ Sixth

Root - 3rd - 5th - 6th
E♭ - G - B♭ - C

E♭6

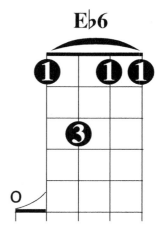

E♭ Minor Sixth

Root - ♭3rd - 5th - 6th
E♭ - G♭ - B♭ - C

E♭m6

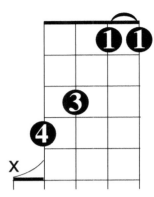

E♭ Seven Flat Five

Root - 3rd - ♭5th - ♭7th
E♭ - G - B♭♭ - D♭

E♭7♭5

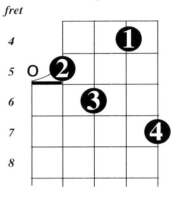

E♭ Major Seventh

Root - 3rd - 5th - 7th
E♭ - G - B♭ - D

E♭Maj7

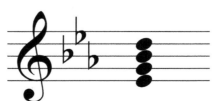

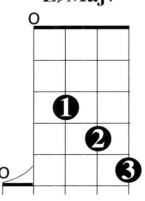

18

E♭/D♯ Chords

E♭ Major Seventh Flat Third

E♭Maj7♭3

Root - ♭3rd - 5th - 7th
E♭ - G♭ - B♭ - D

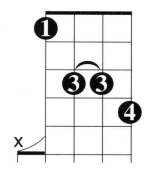

E♭ Minor Seventh

E♭m7

Root - ♭3rd - 5th - ♭7th
E♭ - G♭ - B♭ - D♭

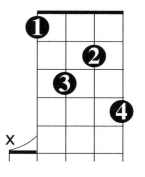

E♭ Minor Seventh Flat Five

E♭m7♭5

Root - ♭3rd - ♭5th - ♭7th
E♭ - G♭ - B♭♭ - D♭

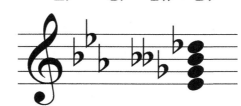

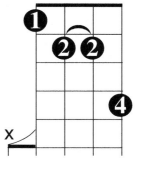

E♭ Seventh Suspended Fourth

E♭7sus

Root - 4th - 5th - ♭7th
E♭ - A♭ - B♭ - D♭

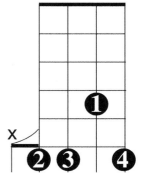

19

E Major

Root - 3rd - 5th
E - G♯ - B

E

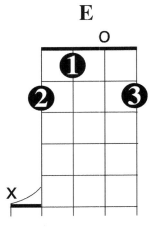

E Minor

Root - ♭3rd - 5th
E - G♮ - B

Em

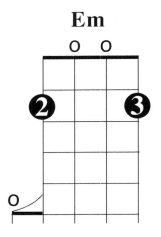

E Seventh

Root - 3rd - 5th - ♭7th
E - G♯ - B - D♮

E7

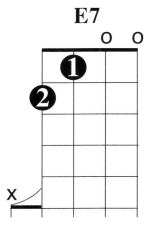

E Diminished

Root - ♭3rd - ♭5th - ♭♭7th
E - G♮ - B♭ - D♭

E°

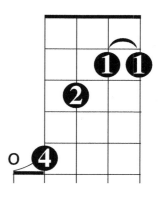

E Augmented

Root - 3rd - #5th
E - G♯ - B♯

E+

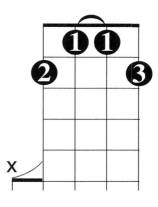

E Sixth

Root - 3rd - 5th - 6th
E - G♯ - B - C♯

E6

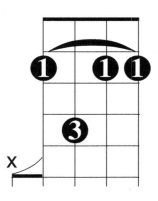

E Minor Sixth

Root - ♭3rd - 5th - 6th
E - G♮ - B - C♯

Em6

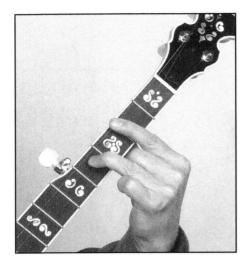

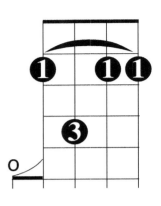

E Seven Flat Five

Root - 3rd - ♭5th - ♭7th
E - G♯ - B♭ - D♮

E7♭5

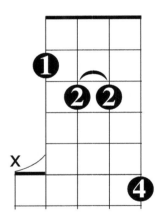

E Major Seventh

Root - 3rd - 5th - 7th
E - G♯ - B - D♯

EMaj7

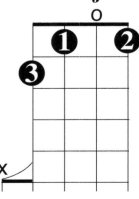

E Major Seventh Flat Third

Root - ♭3rd - 5th - 7th
E - G♮ - B - D♯

EMaj7♭3

E Minor Seventh

Root - ♭3rd - 5th - ♭7th
E - G♮ - B - D♮

Em7

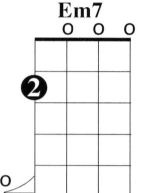

E Minor Seventh Flat Five

Root - ♭3rd - ♭5th - ♭7th
E - G♮ - B♭ - D♮

Em7♭5

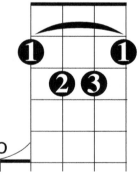

E Seventh Suspended Fourth

Root - 4th - 5th - ♭7th
E - A - B - D♮

E7sus

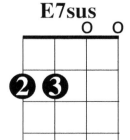

F Major

Root - 3rd - 5th
F - A - C

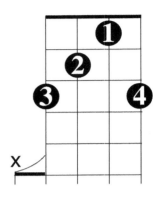

F

F Minor

Root - ♭3rd - 5th
F - A♭ - C

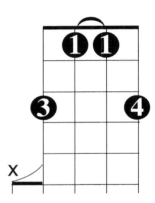

Fm

F Seventh

Root - 3rd - 5th - ♭7th
F - A - C - E♭

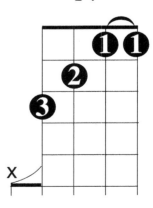

F7

F Diminished

Root - ♭3rd - ♭5th - ♭♭7th
F - A♭ - C♭ - E♭♭

F°

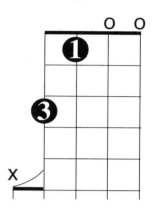

F Augmented

Root - 3rd - #5th
F - A - C#

F+

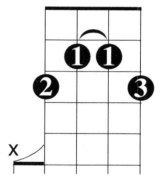

F Sixth

Root - 3rd - 5th - 6th
F - A - C - D

F6

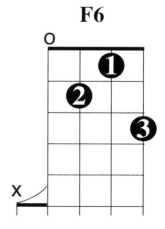

F Minor Sixth

Root - b3rd - 5th - 6th
F - Ab - C - D

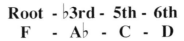

Fm6

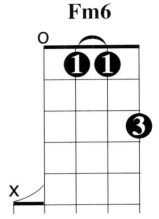

F Seven Flat Five

Root - 3rd - b5th - b7th
F - A - Cb - Eb

F7b5

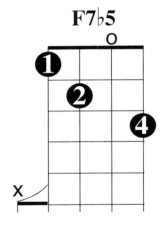

F Major Seventh

Root - 3rd - 5th - 7th
F - A - C - E

FMaj7

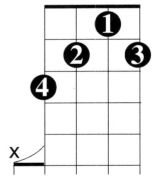

F Chords

F Major Seventh Flat Third — FMaj7♭3

Root - ♭3rd - 5th - 7th
F - A♭ - C - E

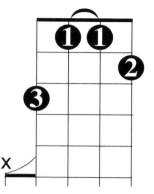

F Minor Seventh — Fm7

Root - ♭3rd - 5th - ♭7th
F - A♭ - C - E♭

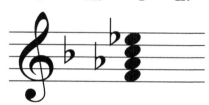
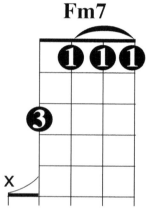

F Minor Seventh Flat Five — Fm7♭5

Root - ♭3rd - ♭5th - ♭7th
F - A♭ - C♭ - E♭

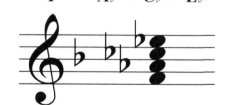
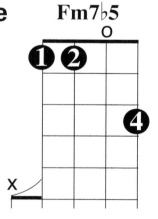

F Seventh Suspended Fourth — F7sus

Root - 4th - 5th - ♭7th
F - B♭ - C - E♭

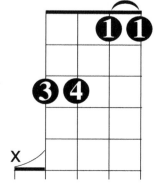

G♭ Major

Root - 3rd - 5th
G♭ - B♭ - D♭
F# - A# - C#

G♭

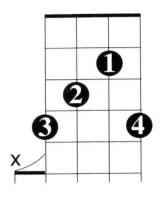

G♭ Minor

Root - ♭3rd - 5th
G♭ - B♭♭ - D♭
F# - A♮ - C#

G♭m

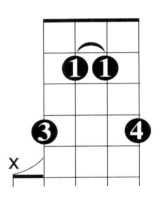

G♭ Seventh

Root - 3rd - 5th - ♭7th
G♭ - B♭ - D♭ - F♭
F# - A# - C# - E♮

G♭7

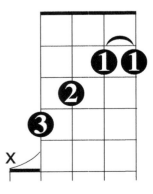

G♭ Diminished

Root - ♭3rd - ♭5th - ♭♭7th
G♭ - B♭♭ - D♭♭ - F♭♭
F♯ - A - C - E♭

G♭°

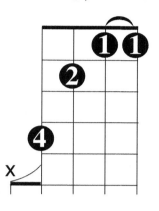

G♭ Augmented

Root - 3rd - ♯5th
G♭ - B♭ - D♮
F♯ - A♯ - C✕

G♭+

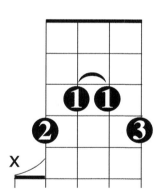

G♭ Sixth

Root - 3rd - 5th - 6th
G♭ - B♭ - D♭ - E♭
F♯ - A♯ - C♯ - D♯

G♭6

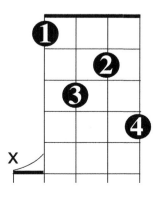

G♭ Minor Sixth

Root - ♭3rd - 5th - 6th
G♭ - B♭♭ - D♭ - E♭
F♯ - A - C♯ - D♯

G♭m6

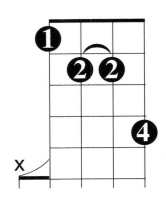

G♭ Seven Flat Five

Root - 3rd - ♭5th - ♭7th
G♭ - B♭ - D♭♭ - F♭
F♯ - A♯ - C - E

G♭7♭5

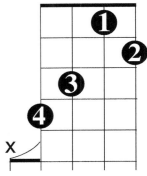

G♭ Major Seventh

Root - 3rd - 5th - 7th
G♭ - B♭ - D♭ - F
F♯ - A♯ - C♯ - E♯

G♭Maj7

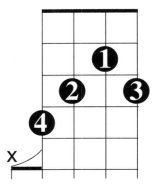

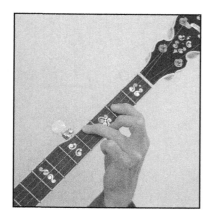

G♭ Major Seventh Flat Third

G♭Maj7♭3

Root - ♭3rd - 5th - 7th
G♭ - B♭♭ - D♭ - F
F♯ - A - C♯ - E♯

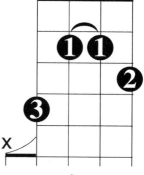

G♭ Minor Seventh

G♭m7

Root - ♭3rd - 5th - ♭7th
G♭ - B♭♭ - D♭ - F♭
F♯ - A - C♯ - E

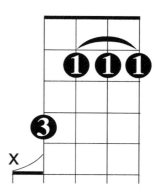

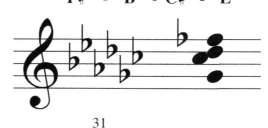

G♭ Minor Seventh Flat Five

G♭m7♭5

Root - ♭3rd - ♭5th - ♭7th
G♭ - B♭♭ - D♭♭ - F♭
F♯ - A - C - E

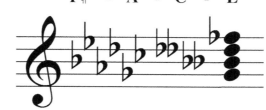
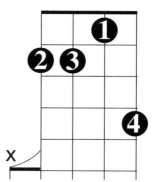

G♭ Seventh Suspended Fourth

G♭7sus

Root - 4th - 5th - ♭7th
G♭ - C♭ - D♭ - F♭
F♯ - B - C♯ - E

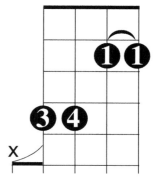

31

G Chords

G Major

Root - 3rd - 5th
G - B - D

G

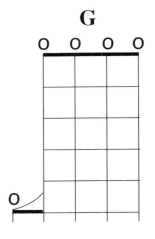

G Minor

Root - ♭3rd - 5th
G - B♭ - D

Gm

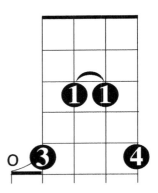

G Seventh

Root - 3rd - 5th - ♭7th
G - B - D - F♮

G7

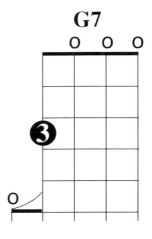

32

G Diminished

Root - ♭3rd - ♭5th - ♭♭7th
G - B♭ - D♭ - F♭

G°

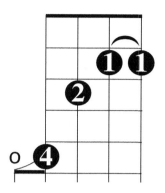

G Augmented

Root - 3rd - #5th
G - B - D#

G+

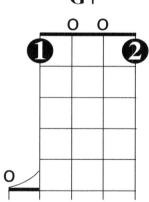

G Sixth

Root - 3rd - 5th - 6th
G - B - D - E

G6

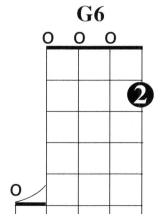

G Minor Sixth

Root - ♭3rd - 5th - 6th
G - B♭ - D - E

Gm6

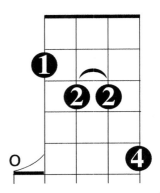

G Seven Flat Five

Root - 3rd - ♭5th - ♭7th
G - B - D♭ - F♮

G7♭5

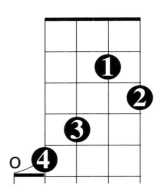

G Major Seventh

Root - 3rd - 5th - 7th
G - B - D - F♯

GMaj7

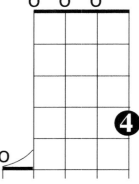

G Chords

G Major Seventh Flat Third

GMaj7♭3

Root - ♭3rd - 5th - 7th

G - B♭ - D - F♯

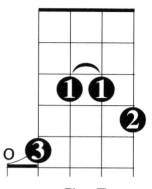

G Minor Seventh

Gm7

Root - ♭3rd - 5th - ♭7th

G - B♭ - D - F♮

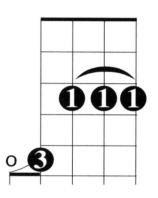

G Minor Seventh Flat Five

Gm7♭5

Root - ♭3rd - ♭5th - ♭7th

G - B♭ - D♭ - F♮

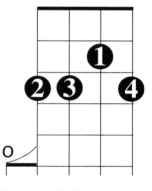

G Seventh Suspended Fourth

G7sus

Root - 4th - 5th - ♭7th

G - C - D - F♮

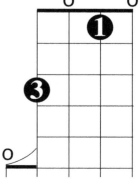

A♭ Major

Root - 3rd - 5th
A♭ - C - E♭

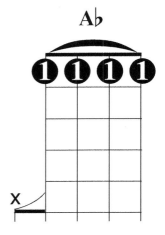

A♭

A♭ Minor

Root - ♭3rd - 5th
A♭ - C♭ - E♭

A♭m

A♭ Seventh

Root - 3rd - 5th - ♭7th
A♭ - C - E♭ - G♭

A♭7

A♭ Diminished

Root - ♭3rd - ♭5th - ♭♭7th
A♭ - C♭ - E♭♭ - G♭♭

A♭°

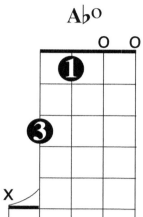

A♭ Augmented

Root - 3rd - ♯5th
A♭ - C - E♮

A♭+

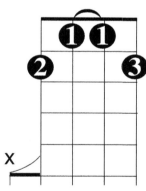

A♭ Sixth

Root - 3rd - 5th - 6th
A♭ - C - E♭ - F

A♭6

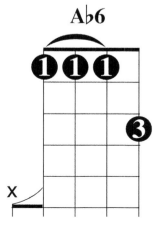

A♭ Minor Sixth

Root - ♭3rd - 5th - 6th
A♭ - C♭ - E♭ - F

A♭m6

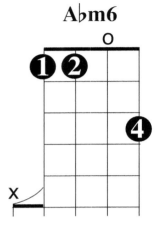

A♭ Seven Flat Five

Root - 3rd - ♭5th - ♭7th
A♭ - C - E♭♭ - G♭

A♭7♭5

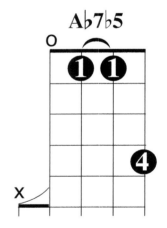

A♭ Major Seventh

Root - 3rd - 5th - 7th
A♭ - C - E♭ - G

A♭Maj7

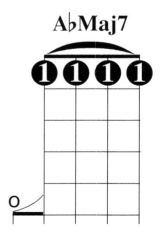

A♭ Major Seventh Flat Third

Root - ♭3rd - 5th - 7th
A♭ - C♭ - E♭ - G♮

A♭Maj7♭3

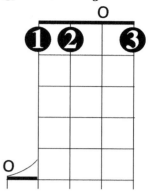

A♭ Minor Seventh

Root - ♭3rd - 5th - ♭7th
A♭ - C♭ - E♭ - G♭

A♭m7

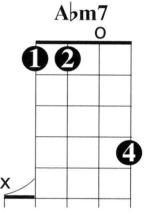

A♭ Minor Seventh Flat Five

Root - ♭3rd - ♭5th - ♭7th
A♭ - C♭ - E♭♭ - G♭

A♭m7♭5

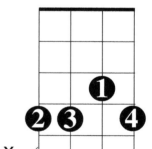

A♭ Seventh Suspended Fourth

Root - 4th - 5th - ♭7th
A♭ - D♭ - E♭ - G♭

A♭7sus

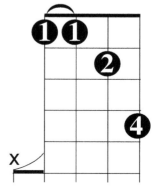

A Major

Root - 3rd - 5th
A - C# - E

A

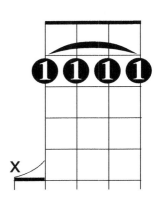

A Minor

Root - ♭3rd - 5th
A - C♮ - E

Am

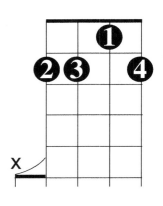

A Seventh

Root - 3rd - 5th - ♭7th
A - C# - E - G♮

A7

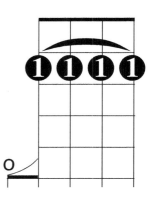

A Diminished

Root - ♭3rd - ♭5th - ♭♭7th
A - C♮ - E♭ - G♭

A⁰

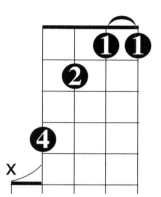

A Augmented

Root - 3rd - #5th
A - C# - E#

A+

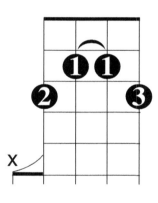

A Sixth

Root - 3rd - 5th - 6th
A - C# - E - F#

A6

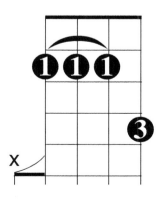

41

A Minor Sixth

Root - ♭3rd - 5th - 6th
A - C♮ - E - F♯

Am6

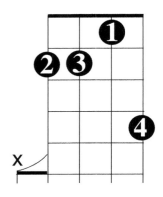

A Seven Flat Five

Root - 3rd - ♭5th - ♭7th
A - C♯ - E♭ - G♮

A7♭5

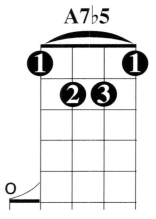

A Major Seventh

Root - 3rd - 5th - 7th
A - C♯ - E - G♯

AMaj7

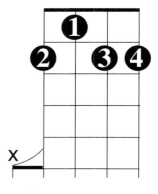

A Chords

A Major Seventh Flat Third

AMaj7♭3

Root - ♭3rd - 5th - 7th
A - C♮ - E - G♯

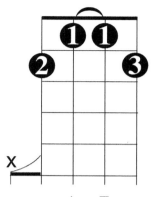

A Minor Seventh

Am7

Root - ♭3rd - 5th - ♭7th
A - C♮ - E - G♮

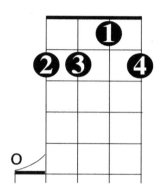

A Minor Seventh Flat Five

Am7♭5

Root - ♭3rd - ♭5th - ♭7th
A - C♮ - E♭ - G♮

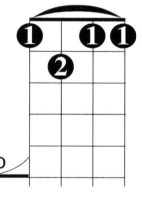

A Seventh Suspended Fourth

A7sus

Root - 4th - 5th - ♭7th
A - D - E - G♮

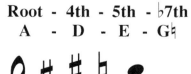

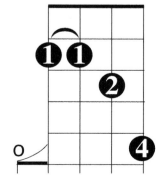

43

B♭ Major

Root - 3rd - 5th
B♭ - D - F

B♭

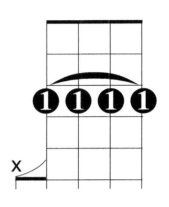

B♭ Minor

Root - ♭3rd - 5th
B♭ - D♭ - F

B♭m

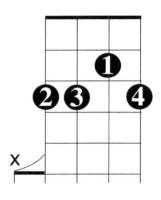

B♭ Seventh

Root - 3rd - 5th - ♭7th
B♭ - D - F - A♭

B♭7

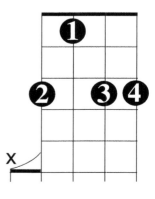

44

B♭ Diminished

Root - ♭3rd - ♭5th - ♭♭7th
B♭ - D♭ - F♭ - A♭♭

B♭°

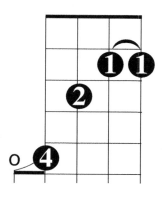

B♭ Augmented

Root - 3rd - ♯5th
B♭ - D - F♯

B♭+

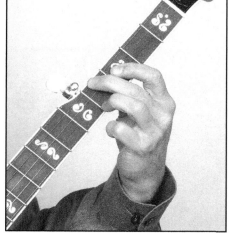

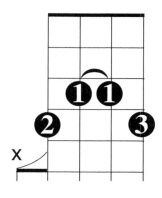

B♭ Sixth

Root - 3rd - 5th - 6th
B♭ - D - F - G

B♭6

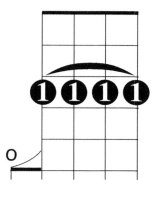

B♭ Minor Sixth

Root - ♭3rd - 5th - 6th
B♭ - D♭ - F - G

B♭m6

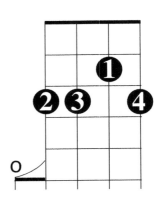

B♭ Seven Flat Five

Root - 3rd - ♭5th - ♭7th
B♭ - D - F♭ - A♭

B♭7♭5

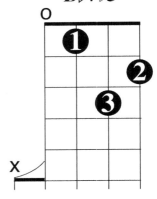

B♭ Major Seventh

Root - 3rd - 5th - 7th
B♭ - D - F - A

B♭Maj7

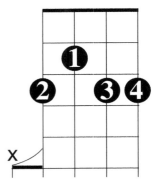

B♭ Major Seventh Flat Third

Root - ♭3rd - 5th - 7th
B♭ - D♭ - F - A

B♭Maj7♭3

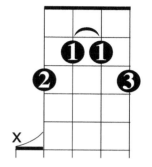

B♭ Minor Seventh

Root - ♭3rd - 5th - ♭7th
B♭ - D♭ - F - A♭

B♭m7

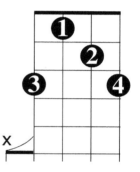

B♭ Minor Seventh Flat Five

Root - ♭3rd - ♭5th - ♭7th
B♭ - D♭ - F♭ - A♭

B♭m7♭5

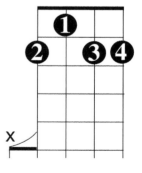

B♭ Seventh Suspended Fourth

Root - 4th - 5th - ♭7th
B♭ - E♭ - F - A♭

B♭7sus

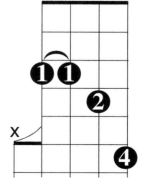

B Major

Root - 3rd - 5th
B - D# - F#

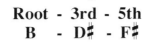

B

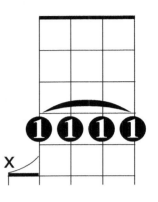

B Minor

Root - ♭3rd - 5th
B - D♮ - F#

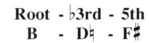

Bm

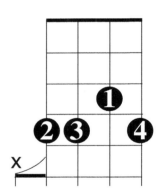

B Seventh

Root - 3rd - 5th - ♭7th
B - D# - F# - A♮

B7

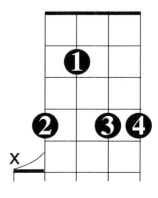

B Diminished

Root - ♭3rd - ♭5th - ♭♭7th
B - D♮ - F♮ - A♭

B°

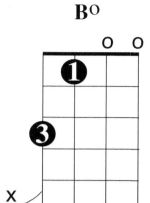

B Augmented

Root - 3rd - ♯5th
B - D♯ - F𝄪

B+

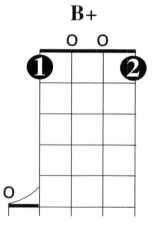

B Sixth

Root - 3rd - 5th - 6th
B - D♯ - F♯ - G♯

B6

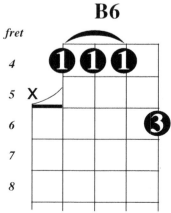

49

B Chords

B Minor Sixth

Root - ♭3rd - 5th - 6th
B - D♮ - F♯ - G♯

Bm6

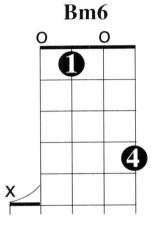

B Seven Flat Five

Root - 3rd - ♭5th - ♭7th
B - D♯ - F♮ - A♮

B7♭5

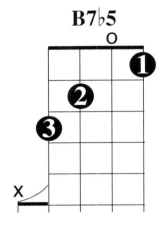

B Major Seventh

Root - 3rd - 5th - 7th
B - D♯ - F♯ - A♯

BMaj7

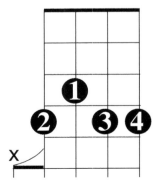

B Major Seventh Flat Third

BMaj7♭3

Root - ♭3rd - 5th - 7th
B - D♮ - F♯ - A♯

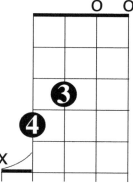

B Minor Seventh

Bm7

Root - ♭3rd - 5th - ♭7th
B - D♮ - F♯ - A♮

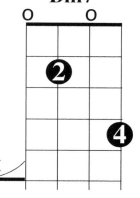

B Minor Seventh Flat Five

Bm7♭5

Root - ♭3rd - ♭5th - ♭7th
B - D♮ - F♮ - A♮

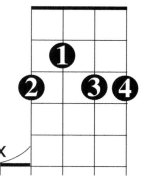

B Seventh Suspended Fourth

B7sus

Root - 4th - 5th - ♭7th
B - E - F♯ - A♮

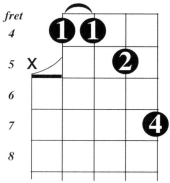

51

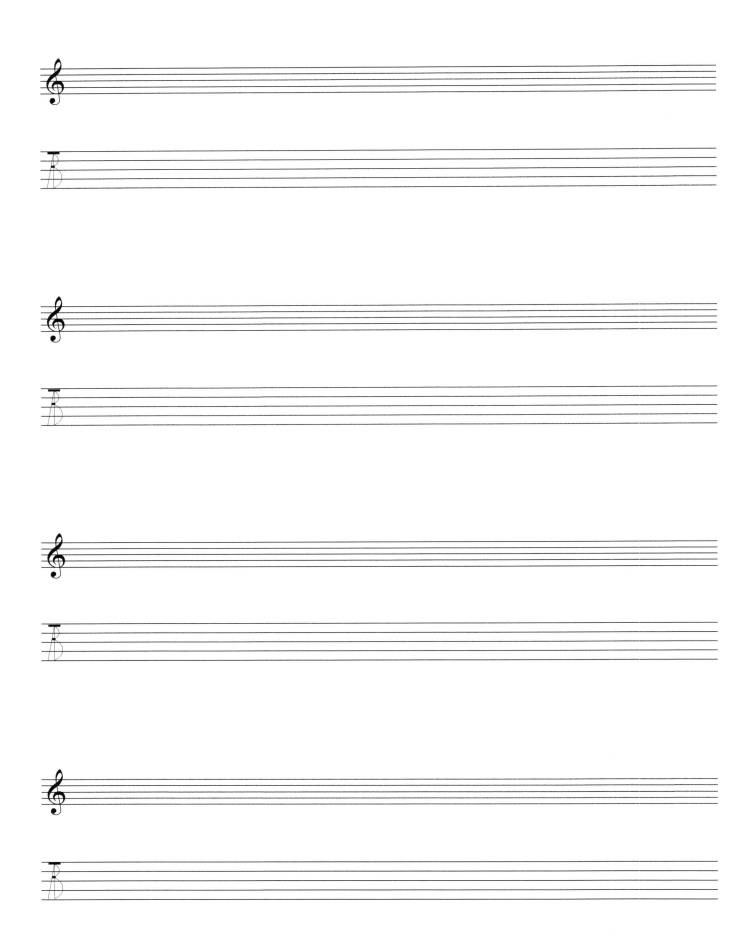

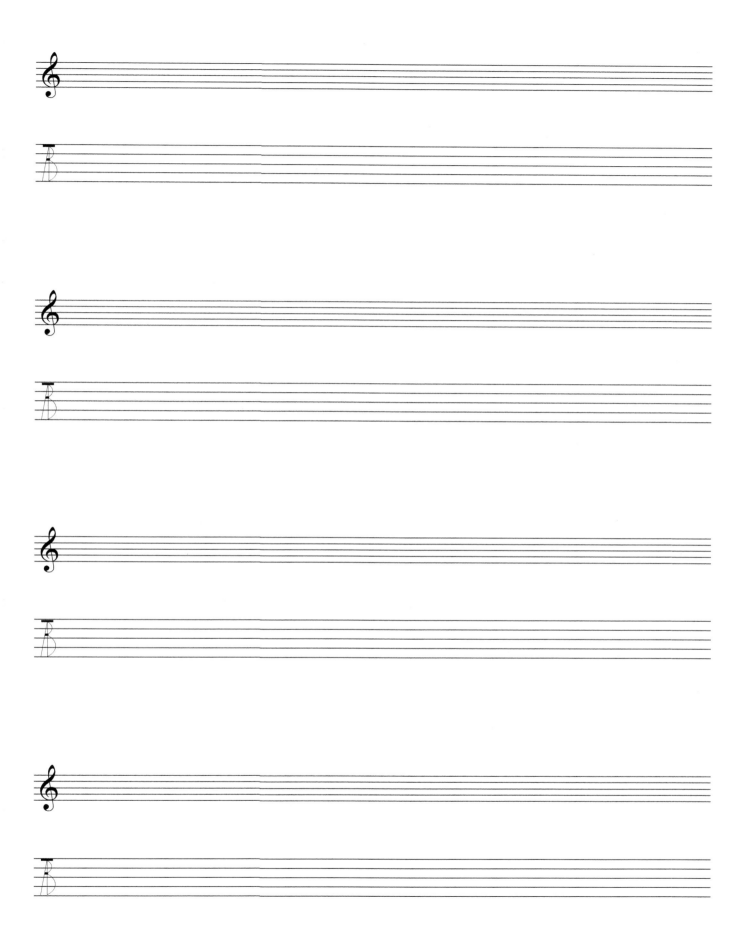

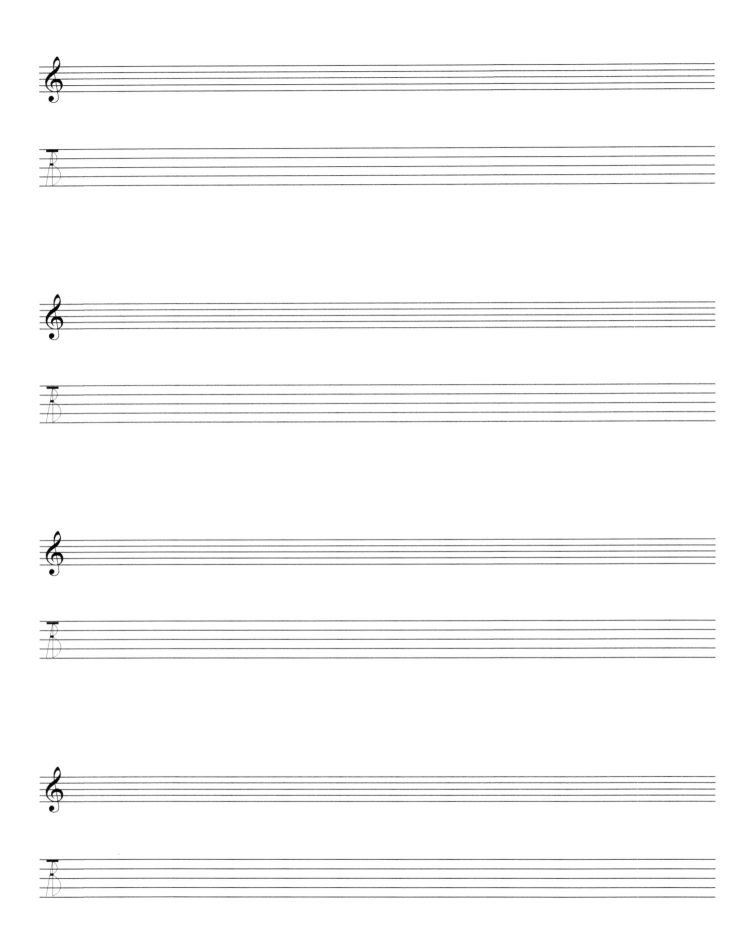

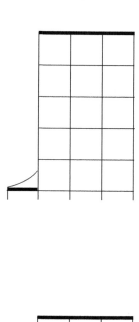
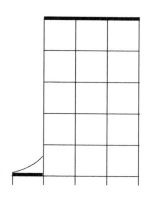
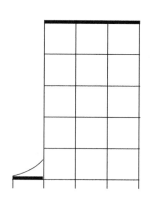
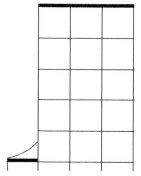
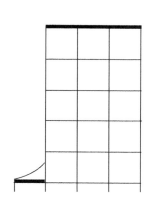
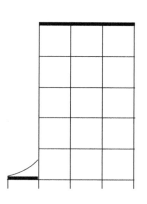
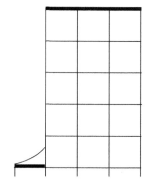
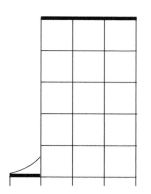
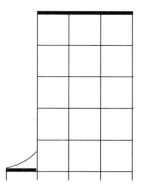

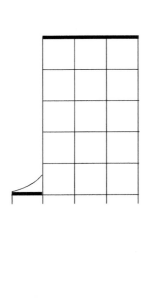
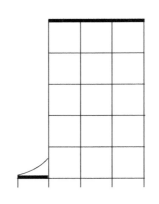
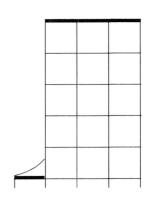
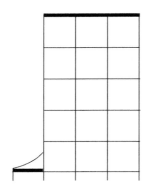
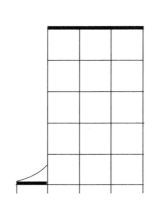
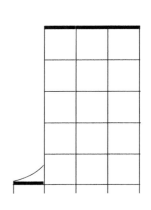
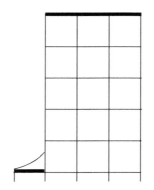
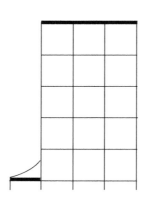
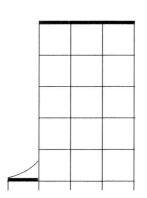

Printed in Great Britain
by Amazon

83858219R00034